SPOTLIGHT ON AMERICAN HISTORY

Thomas Jefferson and the Louisiana Purchase

Sean O'Donoghue

PowerKiDS press™

NEW YORK

Published in 2017 by The Rosen Publishing Group, Inc.
29 East 21st Street, New York, NY 10010

Book Design: Samantha DeMartin

Photo Credits: Cover GraphicaArtis/Archive Photos/Getty Images; p. 5 https://commons.wikimedia.org/wiki/File:Mather_Brown_-_Thomas_Jefferson_-_Google_Art_Project.jpg; pp. 7, 11 SuperStock/Getty Images; p. 8 Chicago History Museum/Archive Photos/Getty Images; p. 9 courtesy of US Army Center of Military History; p. 10 DEA PICTURE LIBRARY/De Agostini/Getty Images; p. 13 https://en.wikipedia.org/wiki/File:Jacques_Louis_David_-_Bonaparte_franchissant_le_Grand_Saint-Bernard,_20_mai_1800_-_Google_Art_Project.jpg; p. 14 https://commons.wikimedia.org/wiki/File:San_Domingo.jpg; p. 15 https://commons.wikimedia.org/wiki/File:Général_Toussaint_Louverture.jpg; p. 16 https://commons.wikimedia.org/wiki/File:James_Monroe_White_House_portrait_1819.gif; p. 17 New York Public Library/Science Source/Getty Images; p. 18 https://commons.wikimedia.org/wiki/File:Louisiana_Purchase.png; p. 19 DEA/W. BUSS/De Agostini/Getty Images; p. 21 https://commons.wikimedia.org/wiki/File:Lewis_and_clark-expedition.jpg.

Library of Congress Cataloging-in-Publication Data

Names: O'Donoghue, Sean, 1984- author.
Title: Thomas Jefferson and the Louisiana Purchase / Sean O'Donoghue.
Description: New York : PowerKids Press, 2016. | Series: Spotlight on American history | Includes index.
Identifiers: LCCN 2015049083 | ISBN 9781508149620 (pbk.) | ISBN 9781508149484 (library bound) | ISBN 9781508149262 (6 pack)
Subjects: LCSH: Louisiana Purchase. | United States--Territorial expansion--Juvenile literature. | Jefferson, Thomas, 1743-1826--Juvenile literature. | Napoleon I, Emperor of the French, 1769-1821--Relations with Americans--Juvenile literature.
Classification: LCC E333 .O36 2016 | DDC 973.4/6092--dc23
LC record available at http://lccn.loc.gov/2015049083

Manufactured in the United States of America

CPSIA Compliance Information: Batch #BS16PK: For further information contact Rosen Publishing, New York, New York at 1-800-237-9932.

CONTENTS

THE THIRD PRESIDENT

Thomas Jefferson was born in Albemarle County, Virginia, in 1743. His father was a **surveyor** and planter who owned thousands of acres of land. He left 5,000 acres (2,023 ha) to young Jefferson, who used it to build a mountaintop estate called Monticello.

Jefferson went to the College of William and Mary. He became active in politics from a young age, serving in the Virginia House of Burgesses and the Continental Congress. Jefferson is perhaps best known for writing the draft for the Declaration of Independence. This important **document** stated the reasons why America had the right to break away from Great Britain.

After the American Revolution, Jefferson served as governor of Virginia from 1779 to 1781. He became a minister to France in 1785 and studied the ways of life there. Jefferson returned to the United States and ran for president in 1796. He lost the election, but served as vice president under John Adams.

Thomas Jefferson was minister to France as the French Revolution was beginning. This was a period of great political ***rebellion*** *and change. It would lead to the rise of Napoleon Bonaparte—a key player in the Louisiana Purchase.*

JEFFERSON'S EARLY PRESIDENCY

On March 4, 1801, Thomas Jefferson was sworn into office as the third president of the United States. At this time, two political parties had recently formed: Federalist and Democratic-Republican. As a Democratic-Republican, Jefferson opposed a strong central government. Many Federalists, such as Alexander Hamilton, were against Jefferson's ideas. Jefferson had to work out solutions between the two parties throughout his presidency.

Jefferson accomplished many things at the beginning of his presidency. He decreased money spent on the military, believing it was no longer as necessary as it had once been. He did, however, send a naval group to fight pirates in the Mediterranean. He also cut the national budget and greatly reduced the national debt. Jefferson's greatest achievement as president was the purchase of the Louisiana Territory, which would double the size of the United States and open the young country to the West.

As a president, Thomas Jefferson believed in treating every citizen with equality. He also believed in the power of education and land ownership.

WESTWARD, HO!

Almost as soon as the United States was founded, its leaders started looking for ways to expand. Thomas Jefferson believed that expanding the United States to the west would be a great opportunity. As someone who owned a lot of land, Jefferson believed that the ownership of small farms would be important to the success of the nation.

Treaty of Greenville

The Northwest Indian War, also known as Little Turtle's War, was a series of battles between U.S. citizens and native peoples between 1785 and 1795. The Northwest Territory included today's states of Ohio, Illinois, Indiana, Wisconsin, Michigan, and part of Minnesota.

American citizens began moving to the frontier, especially the Ohio River and Tennessee River valleys. That region had a great amount of land to be used for farming. The more land they could farm, the greater trade could grow. Unfortunately, this westward expansion led to native peoples losing their homes. The United States waged war with a **confederation** of native peoples for control of the Northwest Territory, or the area northwest of the Ohio River.

As the nation expanded, trade became dependent on the Mississippi River, which ended at the port of New Orleans. Use of the port of New Orleans was necessary to strengthen the new U.S. economy.

SHARING NORTH AMERICA

Until 1803, the United States' territory ended at the Mississippi River. At this time, the land west of the Mississippi River had first belonged to France. René-Robert Cavelier de La Salle claimed the territory near the Mississippi River all the way from today's Canada to the Gulf of Mexico in 1682. He called it Louisiana.

In 1762, near the end of the French and Indian War, France had to give up its land

This artwork shows René-Robert Cavelier de La Salle's expedition to the source of the Mississippi River in 1682.

The French and Indian War in the North American colonies was part of a larger European war called the Seven Years' War. The French and Indian War was fought between the British and French colonies with their native allies.

in North America. Spain received the Louisiana Territory and New Orleans, while territory east of the Mississippi was **surrendered** to Great Britain.

While Spain controlled the Louisiana Territory, it did little to **develop** the land. Its control was weak, so Americans were able to use the Mississippi River and port of New Orleans. Spain's hold on the Louisiana Territory seemed so weak that many believed the United States would be able to acquire western lands in the future.

RISE OF NAPOLEON

The French Revolution completely overturned the social and political systems in France. During the 12-year war, a figure rose to great power. His name was Napoleon Bonaparte, and he **seized** control of France in 1799 following a **coup d'état**.

Napoleon wanted to expand the French presence again in the Americas. In 1800, Spain secretly traded Louisiana back to France in exchange for a small kingdom in Italy. By 1802, France was in the process of taking control over Louisiana—and the port of New Orleans—again. This was bad news for the United States, which needed to use that port. While the U.S. Federalist Party wanted to wage a war against the French, Thomas Jefferson wanted to fix the issue **diplomatically**.

Jefferson did begin to prepare for a war if necessary. However, he also decided to send James Monroe to Paris, France, to meet U.S. Minister to France Robert Livingston. Jefferson knew these two were the United States' only hope for peaceful **negotiation** with France.

In the early 1800s, Napoleon Bonaparte conquered most of Europe. He crowned himself emperor of France in 1804.

IMPORTANT NEGOTIATIONS

Jefferson gave James Monroe instructions to try to make a deal with Napoleon. He wanted to purchase New Orleans to have access to the port. He also wanted all or part of the territory that is today Florida. The United States was prepared to pay $10 million for this very important land.

The Haitian Revolution was a slave revolt in Saint Domingue, a French colony in the Caribbean. Led by Toussaint L'Ouverture, the rebellion was successful in overthrowing French forces.

Meanwhile, Napoleon's France was not as successful as it seemed. There was a threat of a war starting between Great Britain and France. Also, Napoleon had sent the French army to the colony of Saint Domingue (today Haiti), where a massive slave rebellion had been raging since 1791. After the army's arrival, however, yellow fever spread among the French soldiers and many men died. Napoleon's minister of finance, François de Barbé-Marbois, told Napoleon that without control over Saint Domingue, Louisiana wouldn't be as valuable. If France lost a war with Great Britain, Louisiana would most likely be taken over by British Canadians anyway.

Toussaint L'Ouverture

A SURPRISE OFFER

On April 11, 1803, Robert Livingston met with French foreign minister Charles Maurice de Talleyrand. Livingston was willing to negotiate for the sale of just the port of New Orleans and the Floridas. However, Talleyrand surprised Livingston with a new deal on the table. France was willing to sell all of Louisiana to the United States.

James Monroe arrived in Paris the next day and was told of the surprise offer. It wasn't the deal

James Monroe

This illustration shows Napoleon Bonaparte presenting the Louisiana Purchase treaty to United States officials.

they were originally **authorized** to make. However, Monroe and Livingston still negotiated an agreement with France. For $15 million—$5 million more than the authorized amount—they would receive New Orleans and the rest of the Louisiana Territory. This would do more than just give the United States access to its necessary port. It would double the size of the country! The deal was announced on July 4, 1803, exactly 27 years after Jefferson's Declaration of Independence was signed.

THE LOUISIANA PURCHASE

Thomas Jefferson firmly believed in following the U.S. Constitution in an exact way. When he heard about the negotiations to buy the Louisiana Territory, he knew the power to acquire new land was not in the Constitution. He thought about proposing an amendment, or change, in the Constitution to make the purchase legal. However, there was so much support from the American public that Jefferson decided to make the purchase anyway. He knew how important it would be to the future of the United States.

The U.S. Senate **ratified** the Louisiana Purchase treaty on October 20, 1803. Spain had to officially

This painting shows the American flag being raised in New Orleans after the Louisiana Purchase treaty was ratified.

give the Louisiana Territory back to France. Then, on December 20, France gave the Louisiana Territory to the United States. On December 30, 1803, the United States officially owned the Louisiana Territory. It helped to fulfill the American dream that the United States would one day stretch from coast to coast.

THE CORPS OF DISCOVERY

In January 1803, Jefferson sent a letter to Congress asking to fund an expedition across Louisiana all the way to the Pacific Ocean. After the Louisiana Purchase, Jefferson made this plan a reality.

Jefferson sent his secretary, Meriwether Lewis, to lead the expedition. Lewis called upon his friend William Clark to be co-commander. They assembled a group of citizens and military men called the Corps of Discovery. Their goals were to explore and chart the land, make observations of plants and animals, make peace with the native peoples, and find a water route from the Atlantic Ocean to the Pacific Ocean.

The expedition lasted from May 1804 to September 1806. With the help of a Shoshone woman named Sacagawea, the corps found its way to the Pacific and had mostly peaceful relations with native peoples. Journals from corps members contained information on about 122 new animals and 178 new plants. Clark's detailed maps made it easier for more people to move west in the 1800s.

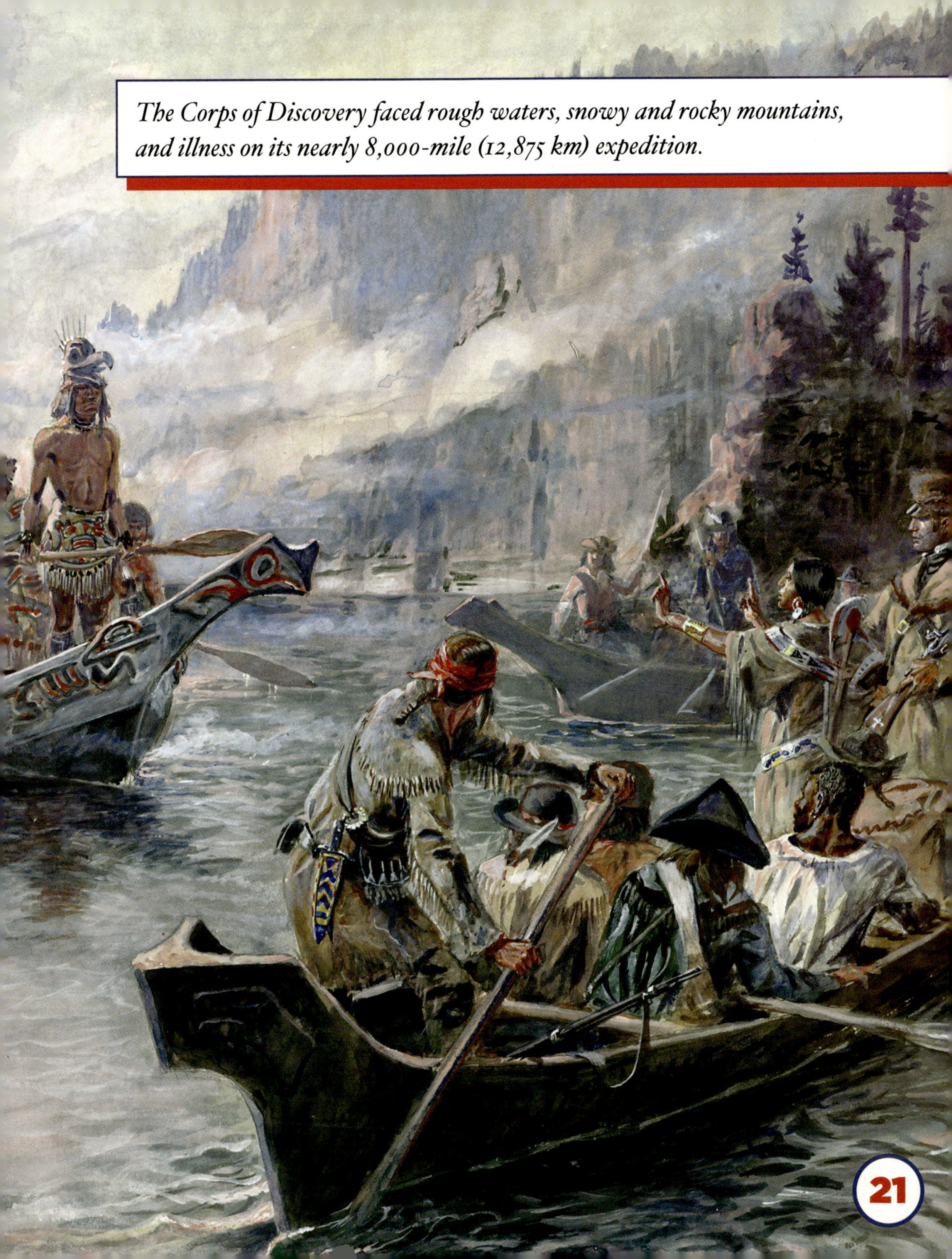

The Corps of Discovery faced rough waters, snowy and rocky mountains, and illness on its nearly 8,000-mile (12,875 km) expedition.

EXPANDING AMERICA

The maps and information provided by the Corps of Discovery allowed more people to explore the Louisiana frontier. Trading expanded and natural resources were plentiful. The land was rich with trees for lumber and valuable metals. Over time, people began to settle on farms out west. In 1862, the Homestead Act gave 160 acres (65 ha) of public land to settlers who wanted to move west. The first railroad that stretched across North America was built in the 1860s.

Thomas Jefferson opened the United States to expansion by making the Louisiana Purchase. The nearly 827,000 square miles (2,141,920 sq km) includes all or part of 15 states today, including Nebraska, Oklahoma, and Kansas. The United States expanded further with the **annexation** of Texas in 1845 and the Mexican Cession of 1848.

Jefferson served as president until 1809. He retired to Monticello and eventually created the University of Virginia. He died on July 4, 1826. Jefferson's involvement with the Louisiana Purchase left his mark on the United States forever.

GLOSSARY

annexation (aa-nehk-SAY-shun): To add an area or region to a country.

authorize (AW-thuh-ryz): To give power or permission to someone or something.

confederation (kuhn-feh-duh-RAY-shun): A league of people or states that support each other and act together.

coup d'état (KOO deh-TAH): A sudden attempt by a small group of people to take over their government.

develop (dih-VEHL-up): The act of building, changing, or creating over time.

diplomatic (dih-ploh-MAA-tihk): Skilled at dealing with other people or nations.

document (DAH-kyoo-muhnt): A formal piece of writing.

negotiation (neh-goh-shee-AY-shun): A formal discussion between people who are trying to reach an agreement.

ratify (RAA-tuh-fy): To give formal approval to something.

rebellion (rih-BEL-yun): A fight to overthrow a government.

seize (SEEZ): To get or take something by force.

surrender (suh-REN-duhr): To give up.

surveyor (suhr-VAY-uhr): One whose job is to measure land areas.

INDEX

PRIMARY SOURCE LIST

Page 5: Portrait of Thomas Jefferson. Oil on canvas. Created by Mather Brown. 1786. Now kept at the National Portrait Gallery, Smithsonian Institution, Washington, D.C.

Page 8: Painting depicting the Indian Treaty of Greenville. Oil on canvas. Believed to have been painted by an officer of General Anthony Wayne's staff. 1795. Now kept at the Chicago History Museum, Chicago, Illinois.

Page 13: *Napoleon Bonaparte, First Consul, crossing the Alps at Great St. Bernard Pass.* Oil on canvas. Created by David Jacques-Louis. Circa 1803. Now kept at the Chateau de Versailles, Paris, France.

WEBSITES

Due to the changing nature of Internet links, PowerKids Press has developed an online list of websites related to the subject of this book. This site is updated regularly. Please use this link to access the list: www.powerkidslinks.com/soah/thom